Peter Nieländer · Sabine Scholbeck

Mein erstes Ravensburger Englisch-Bildwörterbuch

Ravensburger Buchverlag

4 3 2 1 06 05 04 03

Bibliografische Information Der Deutschen Bibliothek
Die Deutsche Bibliothek verzeichnet diese Publikation
in der Deutschen Nationalbibliografie;
detaillierte bibliografische Daten sind im Internet über
http://dnb.ddb.dc abrufbar.

Postfach 1860 · 88188 Ravensburg
Illustration: Peter Nieländer, Sabine Scholbeck
Redaktion: Caroline Jacobi
Wir danken dem Reise Know-How Verlag, Bielefeld,
der uns die von ihm entwickelte Lautschrift für dieses Buch
zur Verfügung stellte. Sie entstammt dem Titel
„Englisch – Wort für Wort", Kauderwelsch Bd. 64.
Printed in Germany
ISBN 3-473-33097-3 · www.ravensburger.de

Content
Inhalt

My body
Mein Körper

face
Gesicht

nose
Nase

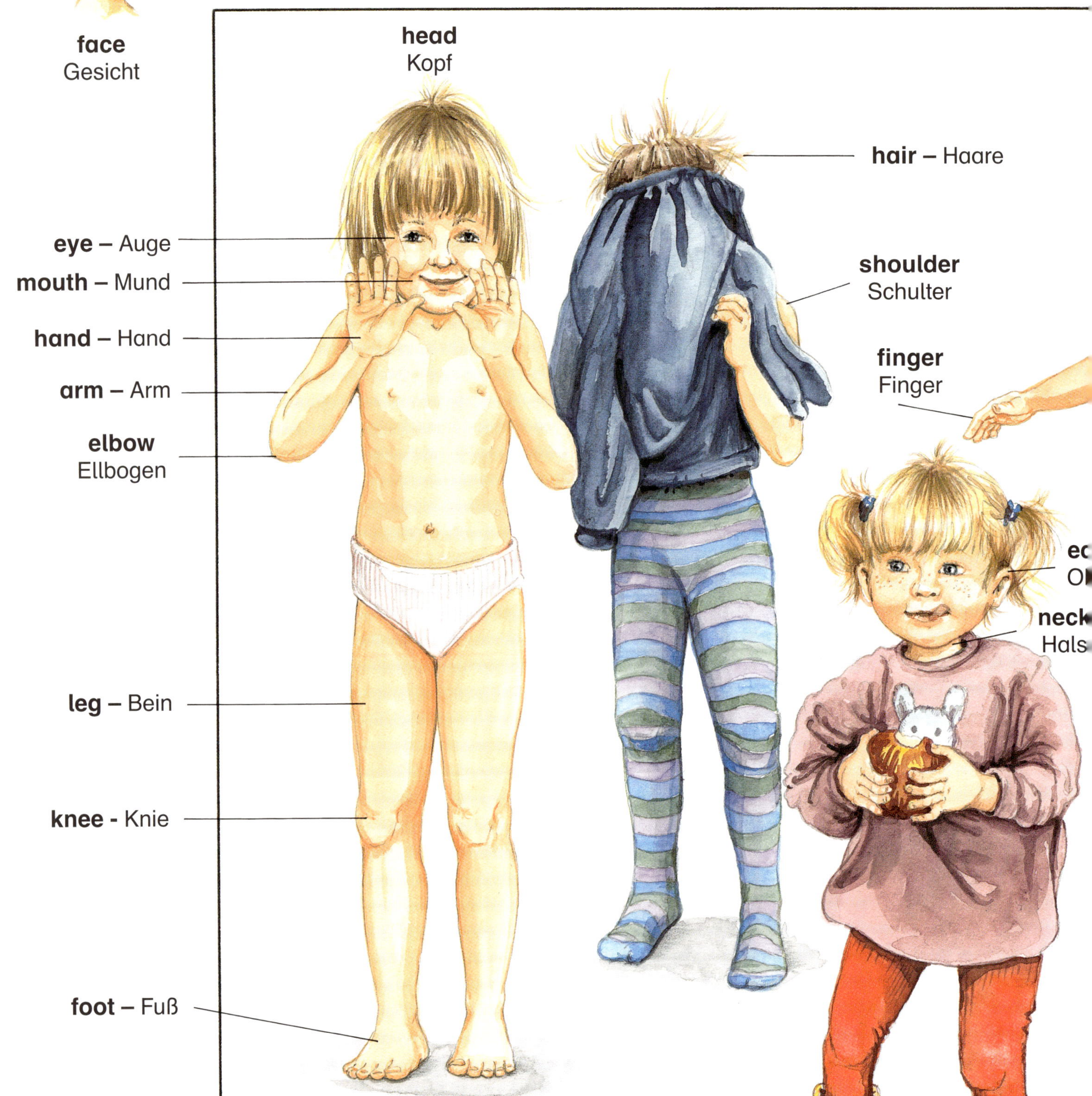

tongue
Zunge

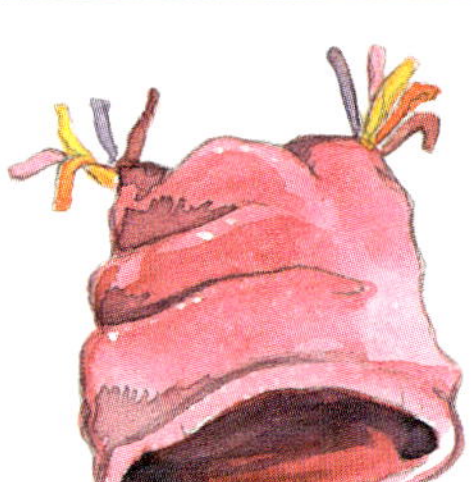

cap
Mütze

anorak
Anorak

button
Knopf

gloves
Handschuhe

skirt
Rock

t-shirt
T-Shirt

rubber boots
Gummistiefel

pyjamas
Schlafanzug

trousers
Hose

dress
Kleid

tights
Strumpfhose

scarf
Schal

jumper
Pullover

belt
Gürtel

shoes
Schuhe

My home – my family
Mein Zuhause – meine Familie

sister
Schwester

mother
Mutter

chair
Stuhl

toilet
Toilette

table
Tisch

dog – Hund

curtain
Gardine

bed – Bett

picture – Bild

window – Fenster

brother
Bruder

grandmother
Großmutter

grandfather
Großvater

father
Vater

sofa
Sofa

lamp
Lampe

guinea pigs
Meerschweinchen

In the kitchen
In der Küche

salt
Salz

pot
Topf

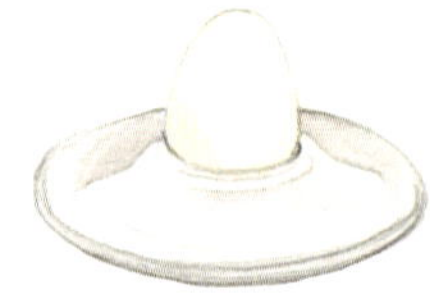

egg cup
Eierbecher

plate
Teller

honey
Honig

glass
Glas

bin
Mülleimer

teapot
Teekanne

orange juice
Orangensaft

butter
Butter

stove – Herd

toaster
Toaster

toast
Toastbrot

fork
Gabel

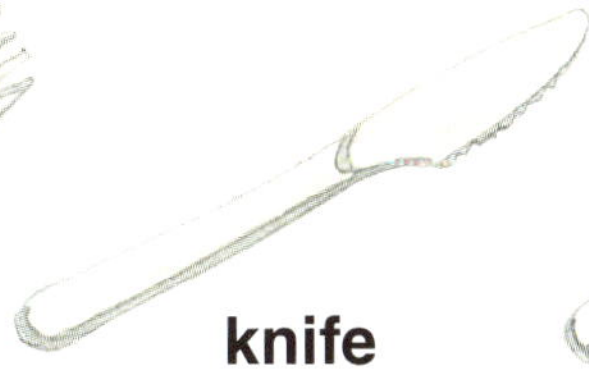

knife
Messer

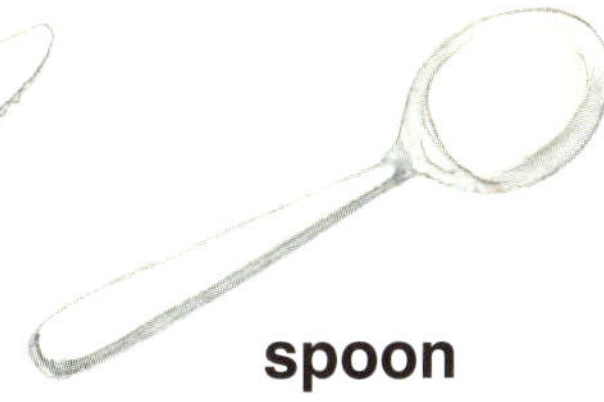

spoon
Löffel

cup
Tasse

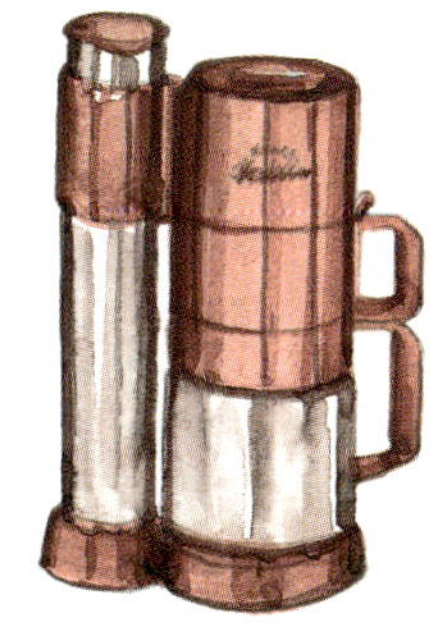

coffee mashine
Kaffeemaschine

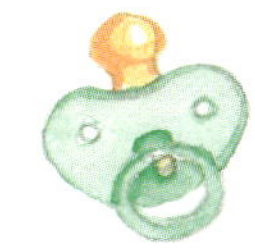

dummy
Schnuller

jam
Marmelade

cornflakes
Cornflakes

dish brush
Spülbürste

sink – Spüle

cake
Kuchen

pan
Pfanne

refrigerator
Kühlschrank

At the kindergarten
Im Kindergarten

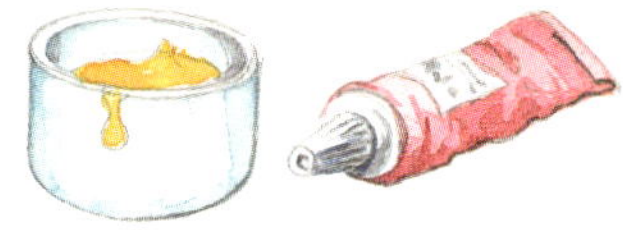

paints
Farben

ball
Ball

friends
Freunde

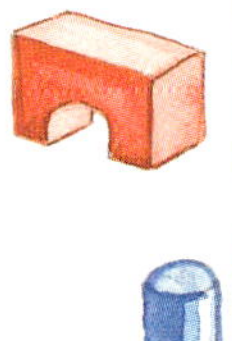

blocks
Bauklötze

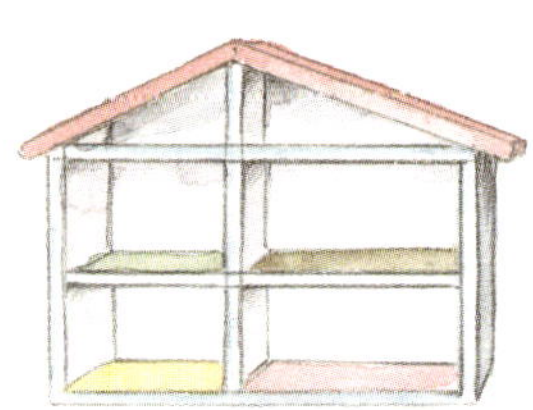

doll's house
Puppenhaus

teddy bear
Teddy

scissors
Schere

toy box
Spielkiste

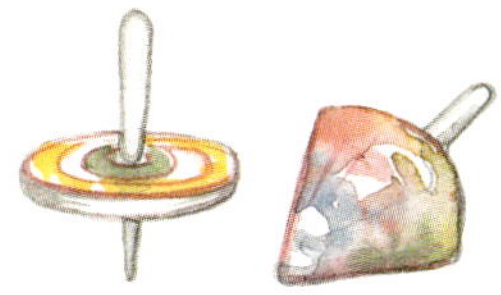

spinning top
Kreisel

puzzle – Puzzle

doll
Puppe

sandwich
Butterbrot

puppet
Marionette

brush
Pinsel

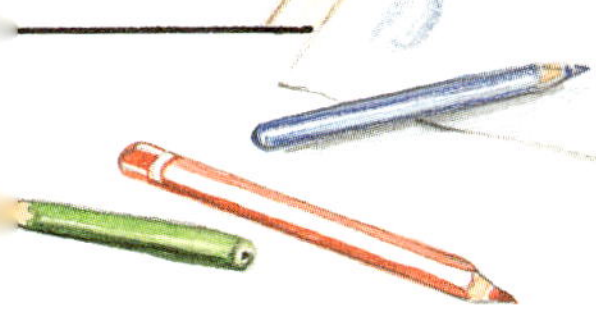

pencil
Bleistift

lego
Legosteine

picture book
Bilderbuch

grocer's shop
Kaufmannsladen

At the farm
Auf dem Bauernhof

appletree
Apfelbaum

barn
Scheune

flower
Blume

goose
Gans

sheep
Schaf

tractor
Traktor

farmhouse
Bauernhaus

grain
Getreide

mouse
Maus

horse
Pferd

cat
Katze

duck
Ente

rabbit
Kaninchen

farmer
Bauer

butterfly
Schmetterling

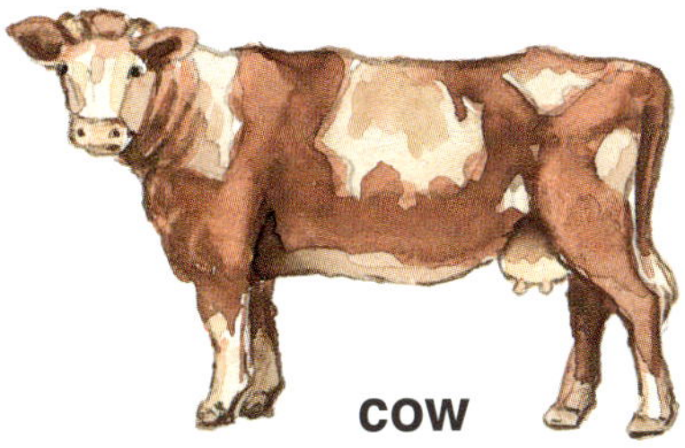

cow
Kuh

chicken
Huhn

wheelbarrow
Schubkarre

pig
Schwein

In the city
In der Stadt

church
Kirche

policeman
Polizist

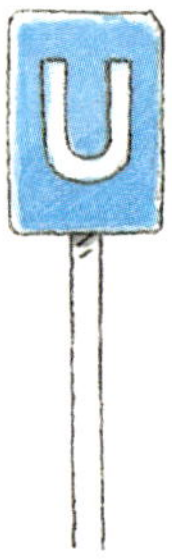

subway
U-Bahn

bus
Bus

street lamp
Straßenlaterne

lorry
Lastwagen

newsagent
Zeitungshändler

motorcycle
Motorrad

skyscraper
Hochhaus

cab
Taxi

postman
Postbote

train
Zug

letter box
Briefkasten

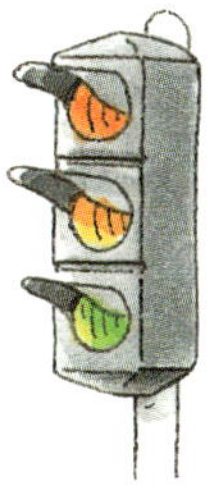

traffic lights
Ampel

clock
Uhr

bicycle
Fahrrad

car
Auto

coffeehouse – Café

tram – Straßenbahn

On the market
Auf dem Markt

carrots
Möhren

fish
Fisch

biscuit
Keks

paper bag
Tüte

scales
Waage

cashbox
Kasse

orange
Orange

ham
Schinken

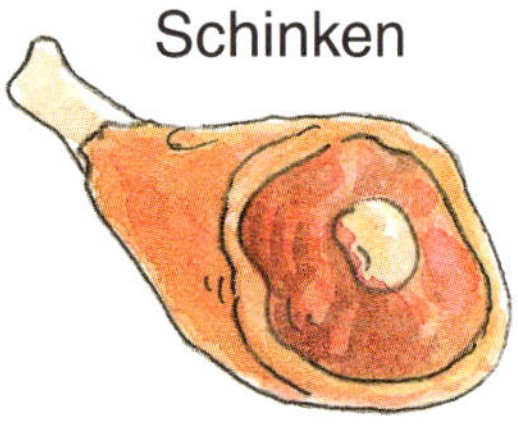

cheese
Käse

cherries
Kirschen

plum
Pflaume

tomatoe
Tomate

eggs
Eier

yoghurt
Jogurt

market woman
Marktfrau

market stall
Marktstand

milk
Milch

potatoes
Kartoffeln

banana
Banane

cap
Mütze

apple
Apfel

bread
Brot

The airport
Der Flughafen

helicopter
Hubschrauber

fire-engine
Feuerwehrwagen

pilot
Pilot

camera
Fotoapparat

teddy bear
Teddy

follow me
Leitfahrzeug

newspaper
Zeitung

suitcase
Koffer

baggage
Gepäck

airplane
Flugzeug

tower
Kontroll-
turm

stewardess
Stewardess

ear-flaps
Ohrenschützer

bagpack
Rucksack

mobile
Handy

sunglasses
Sonnenbrille

tanklorry
Tankwagen

ticket
Flugticket

gangway
Gangway

Animals
Tiere

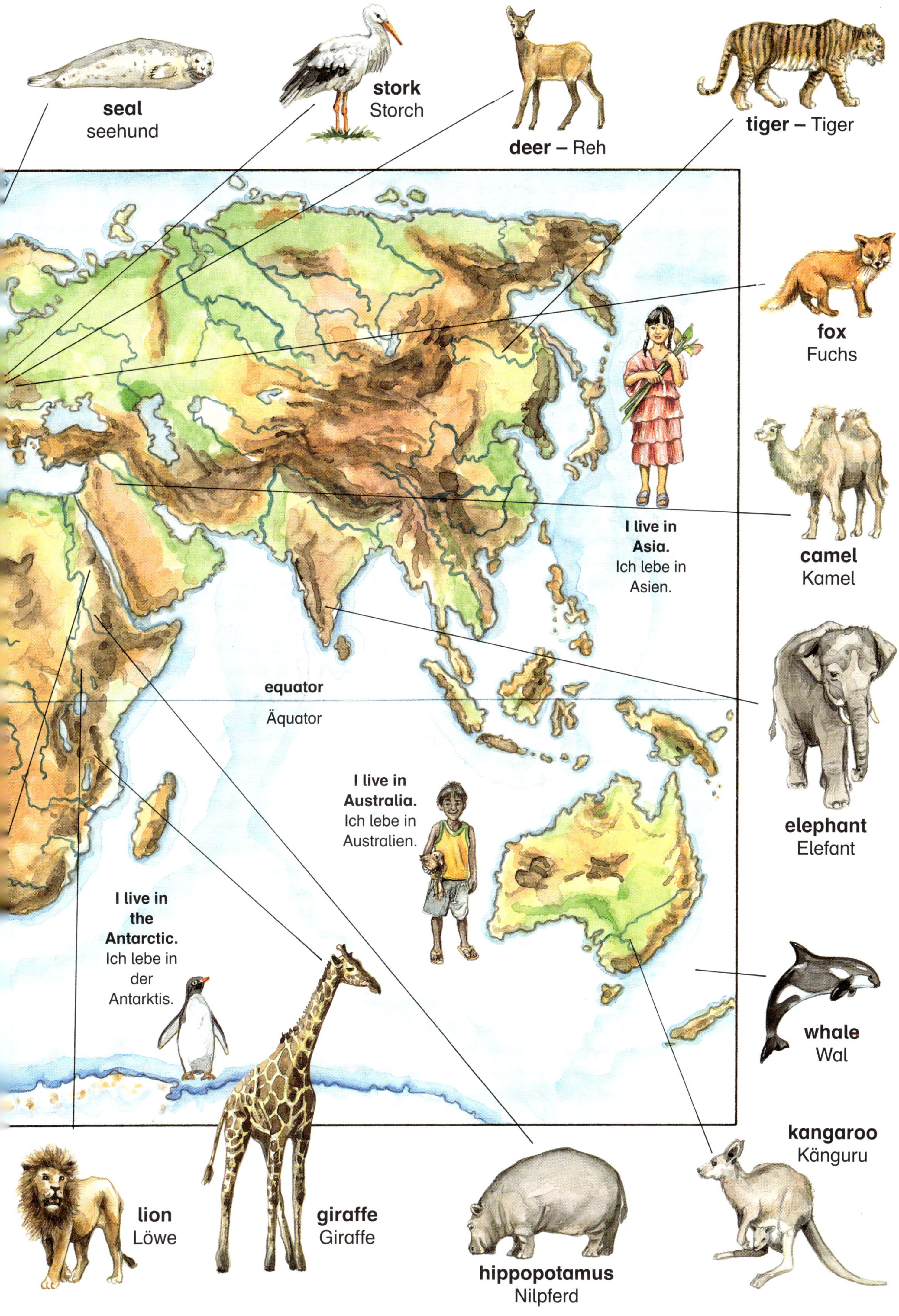
seal
seehund
stork
Storch
deer – Reh
tiger – Tiger
fox
Fuchs
I live in Asia.
Ich lebe in Asien.
camel
Kamel
equator
Äquator
elephant
Elefant
I live in Australia.
Ich lebe in Australien.
I live in the Antarctic.
Ich lebe in der Antarktis.
whale
Wal
kangaroo
Känguru
lion
Löwe
giraffe
Giraffe
hippopotamus
Nilpferd

Seasons
Jahreszeiten

ice cream
Eis

sun
sonne

bird
Vogel

scarecrow
Vogelscheuche

daisies
Gänseblümchen

easter-bunny
Osterhase

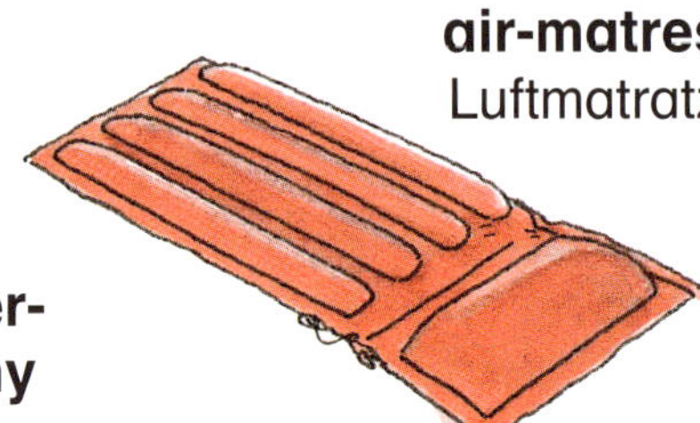

air-matress
Luftmatratze

ship
Schiff

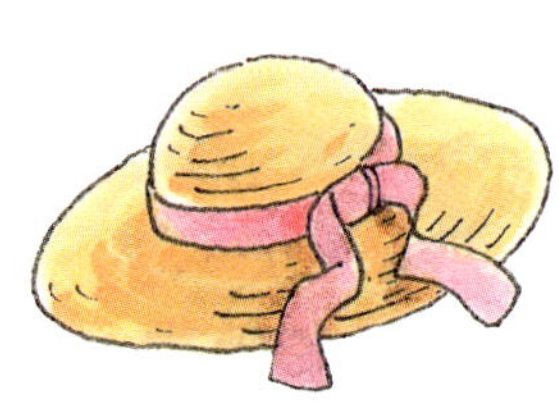

sunhat
Sonnenhut

cloud
Wolke

umbrella
Regenschirm

mountain
Berg

Santa Claus
Nikolaus

christmas tree
Weihnachtsbaum

candle
Kerze

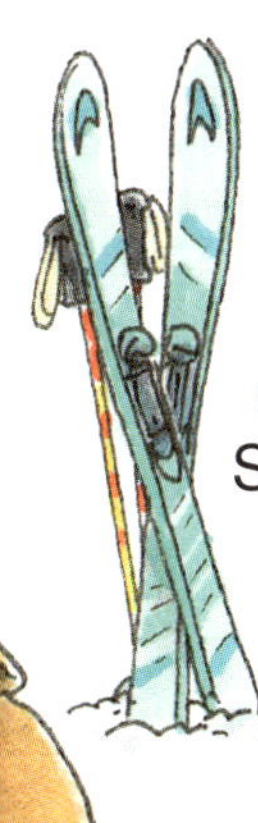

ski
Skier

raincoat
Regenmantel

puddle
Pfütze

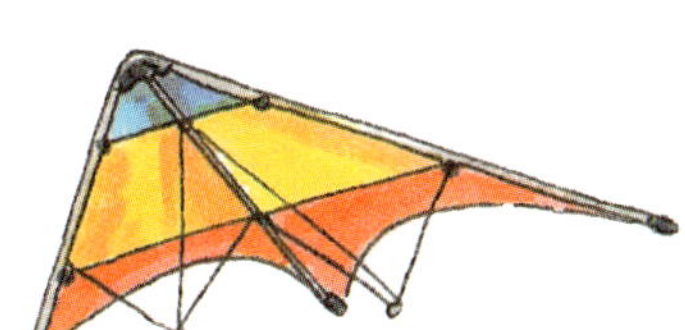

kite
Drachen

present
Geschenk

snowman
Schneemann

What I like
Was ich mag

to run
laufen

to read
lesen

to draw
malen

to talk
reden

to laugh
lachen

to write
schreiben

to embrace someone
jemanden umarmen

to kiss
küssen

to throw
werfen

to hide
verstecken

to swim
schwimmen

to watch TV
fernsehen
to dream
träumen
to sleep
schlafen
to stroke
streicheln
to eat
essen
to drink
trinken
to hear music
Musik hören
to sing
singen
to climb
klettern
to seek
suchen
to play football
Fußball spielen

Numbers
Zahlen

one black panther
ein schwarzer Panter

two white geese
zwei weiße Gänse

three grey donkeys
drei graue Esel

four pink pigs
vier rosa Schweine

five red hearts
fünf rote Herzen

six yellow bananas
sechs gelbe Bananen

seven green frogs
sieben grüne Frösche

eight blue tricots
acht blaue Trikots

nine violett flowers
neun violette Blumen

ten brown eggs
zehn braune Eier

Opposites
Gegensätze

big
groß

small
klein

clean
sauber

dirty
schmutzig

fat
dick

thin
dünn

old
alt

new
neu

up
oben

happy
fröhlich

sad
traurig

open
offen

closed
geschlossen

light
hell

dark
dunkel

sweet
süß

sour
sauer

down
unten

Professions
Berufe

astronaut
Astronaut

captain
Kapitän

hairdresser
Frisörin

veterinary
Tierärztin

ballet danceuse
Balletttänzerin

fire-worker
Feuerwehrmann

reporter
Reporterin

actress
Schauspielerin

animal trainer
Dompteur

doctor
Arztin

football player
Fußballspieler

First dialogues
Erste Gespräche

Wörterverzeichnis

Die Lautschrift in den [ ] – Klammern ist ganz einfach, denn hier werden unsere deutschen Buchstaben verwendet. Ihr müsst also nur das lesen, was da steht und schon sprecht ihr Englisch. Das „ð“ steht für den typisch englischen Lispellaut. Lasst euch den von einem Erwachsenen, der schon Englisch kann, einmal vorsprechen. Das „è“ wird wie ein ganz kurzes „ö“ ausgesprochen. Viel Spaß!

A

actress	[äktrèß]	Schaupielerin
Africa	[äfrika]	Afrika
airplane	[ährpläin]	Flugzeug
airport	[ährport]	Flughafen
alligator	[äligäitè]	Alligator
animal	[änimèl]	Tier
animal trainer	[änimèl träinèr]	Dompteur
anorak	[änèräk]	Anorak
Antarctic	[äntahktick]	Antarktis
apple	[äppèl]	Apfel
appletree	[äppèltrih]	Apfelbaum
arm	[ahm]	Arm
Asia	[äischa]	Asien
astronaut	[ästrènaut]	Astronaut
autumn	[ohtèmm]	Herbst

B

baggage	[bäggidsch]	Gepäck
bagpack	[bägpäck]	Rucksack
balcony	[bälkèni]	Balkon
ball	[bohl]	Ball
ballet-danceuse	[bällèttdänßös]	Balletttänzerin
banana	[bènäna]	Banane
barn	[bahn]	Scheune
bathroom	[baðruhm]	Badezimmer
bedroom	[bädruhm]	Schlafzimmer
belt	[bält]	Gürtel
bicycle	[beißikèl]	Fahrrad
big	[bigg]	groß
bin	[binn]	Mülleimer
bird	[böhrd]	Vogel
biscuit	[bißkit]	Keks
black	[bläck]	schwarz
block	[block]	Bauklotz
blue	[bluh]	blau
body	[bodih]	Körper
bottom	[bottèm]	Po
bread	[bredd]	Brot
brother	[braðèr]	Bruder
brown	[braun]	braun
brown bear	[braun bähr]	Braunbär
brush	[brasch]	Pinsel
bus	[baß]	Bus
butter	[battèr]	Butter
butterfly	[battèrflei]	Schmetterling
button	[batèn]	Knopf

C

cab	[käp]	Taxi
cake	[käik]	Kuchen
camel	[kämmèl]	Kamel
camera	[kämmèra]	Fotoapparat
candle	[kändel]	Kerze
cap	[käp]	Mütze
captain	[käptèn]	Kapitän
car	[kah]	Auto
carrot	[kärrèt]	Mohrrübe
cashbox	[käschbocks]	Kasse
cat	[kät]	Katze
cellar	[ßellèr]	Keller
chair	[tschär]	Stuhl
cheese	[tschihs]	Käse
cherry	[tscherri]	Kirsche
chicken	[tschickèn]	Huhn
children	[tschildrèn]	Kinder
children's room	[tschildrèns ruhm]	Kinderzimmer
christmas tree	[krißmèßtrih]	Weihnachtsbaum
church	[tschörtsch]	Kirche
city	[ßitih]	Stadt
clean	[klihn]	sauber
climb	[klaim]	klettern
clock	[klock]	Uhr
closed	[klousd]	geschlossen
clothes	[klouðiß]	Kleidung
cloud	[klaud]	Wolke
coffeehouse	[koffihhaus]	Café
coffee mashine	[koffih mèschihn]	Kaffemaschine
cornflakes	[kohrnfläikß]	Cornflakes
cow	[kau]	Kuh
cup	[kap]	Tasse
curtain	[köhrtèn]	Gardine

D

daisy	[däisih]	Gänseblümchen
dark	[dahk]	dunkel
deer	[dihr]	Reh
dialogue	[deièlog]	Gespräch
dirty	[dörtih]	schmutzig
dish brush	[disch brasch]	Spülbürste
doctor	[doktèr]	Arzt
dog	[dogg]	Hund
doll	[doll]	Puppe
doll's house	[dollßhauß]	Puppenhaus
dolphin	[dollfinn]	Delfin
donkey	[donkih]	Esel
door	[dohr]	Tür
down	[daun]	unten
draw	[droah]	malen
dream	[drihm]	träumen
dress	[dreß]	Kleid
drink	[drink]	trinken
duck	[dack]	Ente
dummy	[dammih]	Schnuller

E

ear	[ihr]	Ohr
ear-flaps	[ihrfläpß]	Ohrenschützer
easterbunny	[ihßterbannih]	Osterhase
eat	[iht]	essen
egg cup	[äg kap]	Eierbecher
eggs	[ägß]	Eier
eight	[äit]	acht
elbow	[älbouh]	Ellbogen
elephant	[älèfènt]	Elefant
embrace	[ämbreiß]	umarmen

equator	[èkwatèr]	Äquator
Europe	[juhrop]	Europa
eye	[ei]	Auge

F

face	[fäiß]	Gesicht
family	[fämilih]	Familie
farm	[fahm]	Bauernhof
farmer	[fahmèr]	Bauer
farmhouse	[fahmhauß]	Bauernhaus
fat	[fätt]	dick
father	[fahðèr]	Vater
finger	[fingèr]	Finger
fire-engine	[faierendschin]	Feuerwehrwagen
fire-worker	[faierwörkèr]	Feuerwehrmann
fish	[fisch]	Fisch
five	[feif]	fünf
flower	[flauèr]	Blume
follow me	[follohmih]	Leitfahrzeug
foot	[futt]	Fuß
football player	[futbohlpläier]	Fußballspieler
fork	[fohrk]	Gabel
four	[fohr]	vier
fox	[fockß]	Fuchs
friends	[fränndß]	Freunde
frog	[frogg]	Frosch

G

gangway	[gängwäi]	Gangway
giraffe	[dschirahf]	Giraffe
glass	[glahß]	Glas
gloves	[glafs]	Handschuhe
Good-bye	[gudd bei]	Auf Wiedersehen
goose	[guhs]	Gans
grain	[gräin]	Getreide
grandfather	[grändfaðèr]	Großvater
grandmother	[grändmoðèr]	Großmutter
green	[grihn]	grün
grey	[gräi]	grau
grocer's shop	[groußèrß schopp]	Kaufmannsladen
guinnea pig	[ginni pigg]	Meerschweinchen

H

hair	[hähr]	Haare
hairdresser	[härdreßer]	Friseur
ham	[hämm]	Schinken
hand	[händ]	Hand
happy	[häppi]	fröhlich
head	[hädd]	Kopf
hear music	[hihr mjusick]	Musik hören
heart	[hahrt]	Herz
helicopter	[helikoptèr]	Hubschrauber
Hello!	[hälloh]	Hallo!
hide	[haid]	verstecken
hippopotamus	[hipopotèmuß]	Nilpferd
home	[houhm]	Zuhause
honey	[hanni]	Honig
horse	[horß]	Pferd
house	[haus]	Haus
How are you?	[hau ah juh]	Wie geht es dir?

I

I am hungry	[ai ämm hangrih]	Ich habe Hunger
I am thirsty	[ai ämm ðörstih]	Ich habe Durst
ice cream	[aiß krihm]	Eis
I live in …	[ei liw in]	Ich lebe in …

J

jam	[dschämm]	Marmelade
jumper	[dschampèr]	Pullover

K

kangaroo	[kängèruh]	Känguru
kindergarten	[kindergahrdèn]	Kindergarten
kiss	[kiß]	küssen
kitchen	[kitschèn]	Küche
kite	[keit]	Drachen
knee	[nih]	Knie
knife	[naif]	Messer

L

lama	[lama]	Lama
laugh	[lahf]	lachen
leg	[lägg]	Bein
lego	[lego]	Legosteine
letter box	[lättèrbockß]	Briefkasten
light	[laiht]	hell
lion	[leièn]	Löwe
lips	[lippß]	Lippen
livingroom	[liwingruhm]	Wohnzimmer
lorry	[lorrih]	Lastwagen

M

market	[mahkèt]	Markt
market stall	[maketstohll]	Marktstand
market woman	[maketwomän]	Marktfrau
milk	[milk]	Milch
mobile	[moubeil]	Handy
monkey	[mankih]	Affe
mother	[maðèr]	mutter
motorcycle	[motorßeikel]	Motorrad
mountain	[mauntèn]	Berg
mouse	[mauß]	Maus
mouth	[mauð]	Mund
My name is …	[mai neim iß …]	Ich heiße …

N

neck	[näck]	Hals
new	[njuh]	neu
newsagent	[njuhsäidschènt]	Zeitungshändler
newspaper	[njuspäiper]	Zeitung
nine	[nein]	neun
North America	[nohrðèmärika]	Nordamerika
nose	[nous]	Nase
number	[nambèr]	Zahl

O

old	[ould]	alt
one	[wann]	eins
open	[oupèn]	offen
opposite	[oppositt]	Gegensatz
orange	[orèndsch]	Orange
orange juice	[orèndsch dschuhß]	Orangensaft

P

paints	[päintß]	Farben
pan	[pänn]	Pfanne
panther	[pantèr]	Panther
paper bag	[päiperbägg]	Papiertüte
parrot	[pärètt]	Papagei
pelican	[pälihkènn]	Pelikan
pencil	[pänßl]	Stift
penguin	[pängwinn]	Pinguin
picture	[piktschèr]	Bild
picture book	[piktschèbuck]	Bilderbuch
pig	[pigg]	Schwein
pilot	[pailèt]	Pilot
pink	[pinck]	rosa
plate	[pläit]	Teller
play football	[pläi futtbohll]	Fußball spielen
plum	[plamm]	Pflaume

polarbeer	[polahbähr]	Eisbär
policeman	[polißmänn]	Polizist
postman	[poustmänn]	Postbote
pot	[pott]	Topf
potatoe	[potäitoh]	Kartoffel
present	[präsent]	Geschenk
profession	[profeschèn]	Beruf
puddle	[paddel]	Pfütze
puppet	[pappèt]	Marionette
puzzle	[pasl]	Puzzle
pyjamas	[pèdschahmèß]	Schlafanzug

R

rabbit	[räbitt]	Kaninchen
raincoat	[räinkout]	Regenmantel
read	[rihd]	lesen
red	[rätt]	rot
refrigerator	[rèfridschèreittèr]	Kühlschrank
reporter	[rihpohtèr]	Reporter
roof	[ruf]	Dach
rubber boots	[rabbèrbuhtß]	Gummistiefel
run	[rann]	laufen

S

sad	[ßäd]	traurig
salt	[ßolt]	Salz
sandwich	[ßändwitsch]	Butterbrot
Santa Claus	[ßäntèklohs]	Nikolaus
sausage	[ßohßèdsch]	Würstchen
scales	[ßkäilß]	Waage
scarecrow	[ßkärkrau]	Vogelscheuche
scarf	[ßkahf]	Schal
scissors	[ßißèrß]	Schere
seagull	[sihgall]	Möwe
seal	[ßihl]	Seehund
seek	[ßihk]	suchen
seven	[ßäwèn]	sieben
sheep	[schihp]	Schaf
ship	[schipp]	Schiff
shoes	[schuhs]	Schuhe
shoulder	[schohldèr]	Schulter
sing	[ßing]	singen
sink	[ßink]	Spüle
sister	[ßißtèr]	Schwester
six	[ßikß]	sechs
ski	[ßkih]	Skier
skirt	[ßköht]	Rock
skyscraper	[ßkaißkräipèr]	Hochhaus
sleep	[ßlihp]	schlafen
small	[ßmohl]	klein
snowman	[ßnohmähn]	Schneeman
socks	[ßockß]	Socken
sofa	[ßohfa]	Sofa
Sorry	[ßorrih]	Entschuldigung
sour	[ßauèr]	sauer
South America	[ßauðèmärika]	Südmerika
spinning top	[ßpinning topp]	Kreisel
spoon	[ßpuhn]	Löffel
spring	[ßpring]	Frühling
stairs	[ßtärß]	Treppe
stewardess	[ßtjuadeß]	Stewardess
stork	[stork]	Storch
stove	[ßtohf]	Herd
street lamp	[ßlrihtlämp]	Straßenlaterne
stroke	[strouk]	streicheln
subway	[ßabwäi]	U-Bahn
suitcase	[ßjutkäiß]	Koffer
summer	[ßammèr]	Sommer
sun	[ßann]	Sonne
sunglasses	[ßannglaßiß]	Sonnenbrille
sunhat	[ßannhätt]	Sonnenhut
sweet	[ßwiht]	süß
swim	[ßwimm]	schwimmen

T

table	[täibèl]	Tisch
talk	[toak]	reden
tanklorry	[tänklohrih]	Tankwagen
teapot	[tihpott]	Teekanne
teddy bear	[tädihbähr]	Teddy
ten	[tänn]	zehn
Thank you	[ðänk juh]	Danke
thin	[ðinn]	dünn
three	[ðrih]	drei
throw	[ðrou]	werfen
ticket	[tickett]	Flugticket
tiger	[teigèr]	Tiger
tights	[teitß]	Strumpfhose
toast	[tohst]	Toastbrot
toaster	[tohstèr]	Toaster
toe	[touh]	Zeh
toilet	[teulett]	Toilette
tomatoe	[tomäitoh]	Tomate
tongue	[tong]	Zunge
tower	[tauèr]	Kontrollturm
toy box	[tojbockß]	Spielkiste

tractor	[träktèr]	Traktor
traffic lights	[träfickleits]	Ampel
train	[träin]	Zug
tram	[trämm]	Straßenbahn
tricot	[tricko]	Trikot
trousers	[trausèrs]	Hose
t-shirt	[tihschört]	T-Shirt
two	[tuh]	zwei

U

umbrella	[ambrälèr]	Regenschirm
up	[ap]	oben

V

veterinary	[weterihnärih]	Tierarzt
violett	[weièlett]	violett

W

watch TV	[wotsch tih wih]	fernsehen
whale	[wäil]	Wal
What I like	[wot ei leik]	Was ich mag
What is your name?	[wott iß johr näim]	Wie heißt du?
What time ist it?	[wott teim iß it]	Wie spät ist es?
wheelbarrow	[wihlbärro]	Schubkarre
white	[weit]	weiß
Who is this?	[huh iß ðiß]	Wer ist das?
window	[windoh]	Fenster
winter	[wintèr]	Winter
world	[wörld]	Welt
write	[wreit]	schreiben

Y

year	[jier]	Jahr
yellow	[jelloh]	gelb
yoghurt	[jogèt]	Joghurt